Quickie Makes the Team!

By Donald Driver

Illustrated by Joe Groshek

© 2008 Donald J. Driver

ISBN: 978-0-615-23461-8

This book is dedicated to my beautiful children

Cristian and Christina

In Appreciation

First of all, I must thank God for the blessing He has given me.

To my lovely wife and best friend in the entire world, Betina. I love you!

Special thanks to Peter Renaldi for encouraging me to write this book.

Thanks to Joe Groshek, Britte Blair, Brian Lammi, Faye Gray (Mom), Inett Jackson (Mother-in-Law), Donald Driver Foundation, Lammi Sports Management, the Green Bay Packers and DCB80 Enterprise, LLC for all your help and support.

Thanks to my family all across the country!

I Love You!!!!!!!

Quickie loved football. It was his favorite sport. He would watch the older kids play every chance he got. As Quickie stood by the fence, he thought to himself, "I can do this. I can play."

Now Quickie was fast, real fast. No kid in the neighborhood could
beat him in a race. Still, the older kids wouldn't let him play football
with them because they thought he was too small.

One day at school Quickie couldn't believe his eyes. There was a sign that read: "Football Sign-Up." Boy, was he excited!

After class, Quickie ran up to his teacher asking, "Miss Faye, Miss Faye. Can I please have a sign-up form to play football?" With a look of surprise, Miss Faye replied, "Now Quickie, you're too small to play football."

Sad and upset, Quickie walked home from school with his head hung low. Sitting on the porch, Mr. Peters noticed Quickie begin to cry.
"Well hello there Quickie," he said.
"Why are you so sad?"

"I really want to play football, but everyone says I'm too small," sobbed Quickie.

"You don't have to be a big guy to play," Mr. Peters replied. "Remember it is what's inside that counts."

Quickie knew that
Mr. Peters was right.
On his way home,
he said to himself,
"I'm not too small.
I can do this. I can play!"

At night, Quickie would dream that one day he would grow up to be a professional football player and play in front of thousands of people. They would all chant his name, "Quickie! Quickie!" as he scored the winning touchdown.

The next morning before leaving for school, Quickie asked his mom if he could sign up for football with tryouts only a week away. His mom answered, "Oh Quickie, you're too small to play football and you could get hurt. Maybe you should think about playing another sport." It made Quickie sad, but still he believed that one day he would play.

As the family was leaving the house, Mr. Peters stopped Quickie's parents to tell them how upset Quickie was because no one believed he could play football. Quickie's parents told Mr. Peters they would think about letting him try out for football this season.

Later that evening, Quickie's dad called the family together. "Quickie," he said. "You're a big boy and if you want to play football, then that's what you should do. Remember, you should never give up on your dreams, but you will have to work hard at it."

So that night at dinner,
Quickie ate all of his vegetables
and drank all of his milk,
just as his mom taught him.

Every day, Quickie practiced throwing
and catching the football with his dad.
Practice is very important
if you want to be great.

Tryout day had finally arrived!
Quickie and his best friend, Bill, made
their way to the football field
as soon as the school bell rang.

Quickie carefully listened to the coach, followed all of his directions, and worked hard in every drill. When it was over, Quickie said to Bill, "That was hard, but I can do this. I can play!"

The next day at school, the names of the boys who made the team were posted on the locker room door. "Hooray!" Quickie and Bill jumped with joy when they saw their names on the list.

Weeks after the tryouts, the team was getting ready for their first game.
As Coach Marvin gathered the team together, he said to them, "Boys, some of
you won't start, but all of you will play. Now let's go out there and do our best!"

Quickie watched the game, waiting
for the coach to let him play.
Time was running out and Quickie
felt bad his team was losing.

With thirty seconds left in the game,
the team needed a touchdown to win.
Coach Marvin called for Quickie.
"Son, we need your speed!"
Quickie knew if he caught the ball,
he could score and help his team win.

As the quarterback threw the ball into the air,
Quickie reached up and made an awesome catch!
The crowd began to cheer.

As he came down with the ball,
Quickie noticed two blue jerseys chasing him.
He glanced over his right shoulder, then over his left.

Picking up speed, Quickie dodged the first player, then made a move on the second. The crowd began to roar even louder.

With the end zone in sight,
Quickie knew he was only 20 yards
away from scoring the winning touchdown!
The crowd jumped and began chanting,
"Quickie! Quickie!"
as he crossed into the end zone.

Quickie felt just like a professional football player. At that moment,
he thought to himself, "I knew I could do this. I can play!"

It doesn't matter how small you are,
as long as you have a big heart.

To kids everywhere…
I wrote this book to encourage all of you to dream big.
You can become anything you want to be.
Remember to work hard and you will succeed.
Never let anyone tell you that you can't do something.
It's what's inside that counts, so always listen to that voice deep inside that says,
"You can do it!"
It really doesn't matter how small you are, as long as you have a big heart –
No matter what you want to be: a sports star, dancer, doctor, lawyer or even president …

Never Give Up On Your Dreams!

Your Friend,

Donald Driver #80